nia *Give back to the Earth by planting trees*… Dawn S., Wasi

, Alaska *Lead sing-a-longs at nursing homes*… Lois S., Owaton

nton, Alberta *Teach handicapped children*

ollada, Utah *Crochet bandages*

P9-ELP-069

., Boulder, Colorado *Give hand massages at assisted living c*

Marylou T., West Vancouver, British Columbia *Help at the "Bo*

" *children*… Chris H., Menomonie, Wisconsin *Serve 300 me*

es from a refuge house to the hospital… Kathy B., Elk Moun

ah *Do errands for shut-ins*… Wilma H., Snohomish, Washingt

rta *Volunteer with disaster relief*… Dan M., Palm Beach, Flor

olumbia *Help homeless animals find homes*… Jeanne H., S

Chagrin Falls, Ohio *Spend time with my grandfather each day*

JR STAND?

horne, Colorado *Volunteering at daycare centers*… Amanda

ornia *Tutor children in English*… Sherrie O., Fresno, Califor

come "pain free"… Katherine J., Richfield, Utah *Rescue sick p*

ach week… Jan W., Banning, California *Offer manicures at nu*

Teresa M., Fairfield, Iowa *Build a garden therapy project*… Al

Start a Power Lunch program at my school… Dave M., Fairvie

Roslyn B., Denver, Colorado *Visit V.A homes*… Lyle B., N

lbert, Arizona *Meet with terminally ill patients*… Kimberly I

Anne N., Lakewood, Colorado *Deliver fresh baked bread to*

fortunate… Lisza G., Boulder, Colorado *Helping women at abu*

ll R., Overland Park, Kansas *Help financially challenged exp*

ma… Lyn S., El Dorado Hills, California *Adopt a Highway p*

ocal school… Molly S., Ft. Collins, Colorado *Supply potatoes*

Evan & Alla!

enjoy

from

Ron, Sam, Rujina

FOREVERGREEN

A WAY *of* BEING

FOREVERGREEN

A WAY *of* BEING

RON WILLIAMS

with
FOREVERGREEN STAFF AND FAMILY

HIGH MOUNTAIN PUBLISHING

Published by High Mountain Publishing
A division of High Mountain Marketing
Katherine Glover, President

Written in collaboration with Dick Parker

Jacket and book design by Burtch Hunter Design

Manufactured in Canada

ISBN 978-0-9823798-0-6

ACKNOWLEDGMENTS

ONE OF the first steps to maximizing possibility is acknowledging that you are one member of a carefully created team. I have always viewed the people that I work with as my equals. We all have different responsibilities, and while I believe in the importance of job descriptions, I always see someone as bigger than just their job description.

I have had many teachers in my life. Some I have liked more than others; yet, they have all been teachers.

I would like to thank and acknowledge the following, in no specific order:

I want to acknowledge our competitors and other direct selling companies. The pie is bigger than all of us. Thank you for your successes and your commitment to integrity and people in general.

I would also like to thank all of my coworkers/colleagues throughout my career for your patience in me, your belief in me, and your mentorship. Thank you for the opportunities.

The ForeverGreen Members/independent distributors for their honest feedback, their belief, support, and hard work in making ForeverGreen tangible. Every day is a personal refinery!

The ForeverGreen team of employees. From left to right, top to bottom, thank you for your consistency and hard work. We *are* like one big family.

The executives and directors of ForeverGreen, for caring enough to challenge ideas, for understanding the power of alignment, and for your openness to personal and professional development.

My executive assistant, Allison, for her initiative in detail, culture, and results, and for holding me up, daily, to an expectation of leadership and responsibility. Truth, without your contributions, ForeverGreen wouldn't be the great company that it is. Never taken for granted.

Craig S. It doesn't matter what you do, it just gets done, in excellence! No stories! You are living results. No job is too big or too small for you. Thank you for expecting me to "show up" every day. Again, never taken for granted.

My business partners John C. and George B., whom I have had the great pleasure of working with, and learning from their wisdom, experience, and success.

Katherine G., President of High Mountain Marketing, for seeing the value in this book and making it happen. For your vision, wisdom, friendship, permanent smile, and commitment to making our industry an industry of quality and creativity.

Dick P. for your adaptive wisdom to the offerings of this book, and for putting your heart and soul into its intent. You have a gift, and I will be forever grateful to have benefited from your writing talents.

My siblings, Chuck, Cheryl, Eddie, and Shelly who truly played a big role in molding who I am today. Thank you for your love, support, and friendship. This would also include all my beautiful nieces and nephews.

My dad, Charles. Thank you, Dad, for being open to making up for lost time. It is all about the day at hand, and I am grateful to know you and benefit from the great traits I inherited from you. I love you.

Oh yeah, Mom, Lynne. What can I say? You are a modern-day hero, and an example to single moms around the world. Your tough love taught me that there was no mountain too high. You are a fantastic mother and grand-mother. I love you.

My newborn daughter, Gema Jolee, for bringing a fresh spirit of love and reinvention into my life. Thank you for your transparency and having no judgment on the events of life. Already, you are teaching. I love you.

Maron. At times I feel guilty, as you have been my selfish indulgence for inspiration, purpose, and success. It seems like yesterday, as a single dad, having you by my desk, day after day in your car seat, reminding me to stay grounded, loving, trusting and committed. Thank you for being unique, special, and full of heart. I love you, Mare Bear.

My wife, Kandi, for making our little family better, and for your unconditional love for Maron and me. For all of the small things you do that add up to big love. Thank you for Gema and for all your time and love invested in her. Putting up with me, I know, isn't easy, yet thank you for seeing past the imperfections. I love you.

God, my creator. Thank you for leading me in spite of my baggage, and making known unto me that it is the journey, not the events. I seek no credit.

FOREVERGREEN

A WAY *of* BEING

HEALTH

KINDNESS

OPPORTUNITY

EMBRACING KINDNESS

We are all connected. If it happens to you, it happens to me.

—
R.W.

"DADDY," my young daughter, Maron, asked, "where's Mommy?"

My heart sank as I looked at my beautiful girl. "I don't know, honey," I said.

I cried that night as I lay in bed. My wife, Nancy, had left us when Maron was an infant, and she had not been in our life in over a decade.

Some weeks later Maron once again asked where her mother was. I didn't tell her that I had not seen her mother in years and didn't even know where to look for her. Once again I simply said, "I don't know."

Over time, the question came again and again, and after a while I knew I had to find the answer. I had to connect the dots in Maron's life. A little girl should know her mother.

Yet I had other major responsibilities. ForeverGreen, the company I founded, had just grown beyond the start-up stage and was quickly gaining momentum. During that critical time in the life of any company, it's "all hands on deck," especially for the founder. Divert your attention even for a moment, and you could soon find yourself against the rocks.

Before starting the company, however, I had decided that ForeverGreen would be different. We would be about changing the world around us while making money. Maron's questions about her mother would put that commitment to the test. The quest I was about to embark on— the stand I was about to take—would demand critical time and resources from the entire ForeverGreen staff and me.

The reward for taking that stand would be greater than anything I could have imagined.

WHY SEEK A HIGHER PURPOSE?

The richest man in history never took a stand, and he died miserable. During his life he built houses for himself, planted vineyards, made gardens and parks with all kinds of fruit trees, amassed a treasure of silver and gold—in short, he denied himself nothing. Yet shortly before he died, King Solomon wrote, "I hated life. Then I hated all my labor."

For him everything centered on satisfying his own desires, and when we work for no greater purpose than that, then joy is as hard to grasp as the wind itself.

R.W.

Take a Stand

We finally found Nancy living on the street—a heroin addict. It was hard for me to imagine anyone in Utah might be addicted to heroin, but I learned that years earlier Nancy had become addicted to prescription drugs, and over time her addiction led her to street drugs, and finally life on the street.

We had to help her. She said she was willing to participate in a recovery program, so I contacted a detoxification center in Orem, Utah, where the ForeverGreen headquarters is located, and learned that the waiting list to get in was months long.

"Come on," I said to the center's representative, "in Orem? That's impossible." Utah has such a reputation for clean living. Then they educated me about what's going on with addiction in our state. Calls to other facilities confirmed the situation.

Before I made those calls, I thought Maron must be the only child in Utah whose mom was a drug addict. Now I was learning there were hundreds, maybe thousands, more. I couldn't keep that knowledge to myself. How many more little girls were asking about their missing mommy or daddy? I had to find a way to share this information, and by sharing, perhaps prevent others from getting caught in the same spiraling bear trap.

What about a movie?

The idea was truly insane . . . and completely transforming. Craig Smith, Dan Barnett, and I sat around a table at a local health-food restaurant and considered the possibilities. Craig and Dan had been producing short corporate videos for ForeverGreen since our founding a couple of years earlier. Dan is an absolute professional behind the camera, and Craig has a passion for making things happen and connecting people, along with a double share of compassion. Neither of them had taken on anything as big as a full-length movie, but with passion, vision, and their capability, we made our plans.

We decided to tell a true story, but not told in the sometimes-plodding documentary style. For a true story, we needed real people telling their own stories, and we would offer other addicts the same help we had given Nancy, access to professional assistance.

We would title our movie *Happy Valley*, drawing attention to the irony that Utah, and particularly the Wasatch Front area from Salt Lake to Provo known by many as

———————————

Some time ago Ron and I were talking about what my passion is. I'm okay working in the day-to-day corporate management, but I'd rather be in a nursing home or filling a Wal-Mart shopping cart with personal CD players for the people who live there. Education also excites me. I work with freshmen at a local university. And I love working with children. So now I am ForeverGreen's director of community stands and managing director of the Happy Children Foundation, which Ron founded. It's a perfect fit for my passion.

CRAIG SMITH, DIRECTOR OF COMMUNITY STANDS

———————————

Happy Valley, has its sad sides. The movie's tagline, "What's in your Jell-O?" speaks directly to the great statistical data we generate in Utah. We lead the nation in literacy. We even consume the most Jell-O. Yet I learned we have twice the national average of prescription drug abuse, which leads to street drug abuse. Of course, people don't live on statistics, good or bad. We have to consider the deeper questions. When we ask, "What's in your Jell-O?" we're really asking, "What are you in denial about? What cross do you secretly bear? What hidden challenges do you face?"

Within twenty-four hours of our decision, Craig was designing a billboard, setting up a dedicated telephone line, and coordinating with drug treatment facilities. We leased three billboards on the highway between Orem and Salt Lake City offering free help to anyone who called. Craig, with his unique sensitivity for the needs of others, took each call. They agreed to meet with us, and many were amazingly willing to take a stand and say out loud, "I have a problem." Watching them on screen, you can feel so much pain—the pain of good people who have a bad habit.

To put the story into a larger context, we knew we also had to interview those who are working to solve this problem. Craig contacted the FBI, the Drug Enforcement

Agency, the Utah attorney general, undercover drug agents, and many, many more who understand the problem.

"It was amazing," Craig says. "Nobody turned us down. Not only did they participate but they also gave us access we never imagined possible.

"We needed to conduct an interview in a jail, and they suggested a tape recorder through the glass. Well, that just wasn't going to work. Then they said maybe we could film through the glass. That still wasn't going to be satisfactory, but we didn't want to push too hard. Finally they gave us full access to do the interview in the same room. When we left that day, the lady working behind the desk at the jail administration area said, 'Who are you guys?' We said we were the *Happy Valley* film crew—nobody, really. 'Well, in all the years of this jail,' she said, 'nobody has ever gone through that door with a camera.'"

The impact of *Happy Valley* was equally stunning.

In June 2007 *Happy Valley* premiered at the Breckenridge Film Festival, which has introduced such acclaimed films as *The Shawshank Redemption, L.A. Confidential, American Beauty,* and *Motorcycle Diaries.* Our film became the hit of the festival, taking the Audience Choice award following three sold-out showings (two more than the original schedule). Then *Happy Valley* was awarded the festival's Grand Prize.

The acclaim was special, but nothing compared with the reaction we witnessed when *Happy Valley* opened in theaters. Craig was answering twenty calls a day and even more e-mails from people and families now empowered to take a stand against their own addiction issues. The governor, attorney general, and state legislature created or enhanced antidrug efforts utilizing the momentum generated by *Happy Valley*.

The whole idea of encouraging people to get outside themselves, find something that gets them excited, and give back to others proves there is something bigger than all of us out there.

BEN ALLEN, DIRECTOR OF MARKETING

This story is certainly not unique to Utah. Drug addiction indiscriminately crosses all boundaries of race, religion, economic status, gender, broken families, or strong

When network marketing leaders visit ForeverGreen, often the first thing Ron does is show them the movie *Happy Valley*. Then he tells them, "Now you know what we're all about and where we've chosen to take our stand." It's not about our product or our comp plan. Everybody has one of those. Ron wants them to know that we're about changing people's lives, and if that's what they're looking for, we're the place.

CRAIG SMITH, DIRECTOR OF COMMUNITY STANDS

families. It could be anyone. We could have flown to Omaha or any other city in America, interviewed a bunch of strangers, and made the same movie. Addictions there may be different—alcohol or street drugs instead of prescription drugs—but each is a unique expression of a similar issue. We told the story in Utah because I believe there is something beautiful and profound about taking a stand in your own backyard. Here we are known for our high morals, standards, and principles. *Happy Valley* reminds us to root those in reality, and the reality is, we have a real problem. The purpose of the movie is to inspire people to step into the question, and it is amazing to see how many people have done just that.

"I ascribe a lot of the impact to a higher power," Craig says. "There are just too many miracles that allowed people's lives to be touched and changed."

Watching *Happy Valley* and seeing its impact, I have to agree. It feels like a miracle. Miracles happen when you take a stand with passion.

Most of us at ForeverGreen came from big companies—corporate environments where it's a dog-eat-dog world and where you often see discrimination by race, color, and gender. As soon as I met Ron and got to know him, I felt at home. Here I am, an Asian woman who speaks English as a second language, and I have this corporate leader who trusts me and believes in my knowledge and experience. That says a lot about ForeverGreen. A lot of corporations look first at the bottom line and see how they can get the most financial return from each person. ForeverGreen cares about each employee and each distributor as a human being first and upholds us at a higher level, allowing us to grow and develop individually.

BRENDA HUANG, CHIEF MARKETING OFFICER

I've been through a number of interview processes with a number of companies. When I met with Ron, he went through my resume and asked all the right questions. He seemed to have an intuitive understanding of my strengths. As he finished the interview, he said, "Now I'm going to do the hardest part of the interview." I waited expectantly, and he said, "I see on your resume you were a basketball coach."

"That's right," I said. "Seven years."

"So let's go outside."

Behind the ForeverGreen headquarters he had a basketball court, and we shot hoops and talked. At that moment I knew Ron was the kind of person I wanted to work with.

PAUL FRAMPTON, CHIEF FINANCIAL OFFICER

LESSONS OF CHILDHOOD

I was never a person to say, "We don't have it."
I'd say, "Let's go get it."
—
LYNNE WILLIAMS
Ron's mom

I NEVER imagined, when Maron was born, that I would soon become a single parent. Not long afterward, though, I began to realize the familiarity of the role.

My mother, whose heritage is Polynesian and Japanese, was abandoned as an infant and raised as a foster child by a minister and his wife. They died when she was thirteen years old, and she was sent to a boarding school. My father, tall and fair, the son of German and Welsh parents, saw this small, beautiful young woman and fell in love with her. They married, and by the time she was twenty-two years old, Mom was living alone in Southern California with four children. My father had gone. Mom had no parents, brothers, sisters, aunts, uncles, or cousins who might support her, and no skills to earn more than minimum wage. She was simply a mother.

Mom worked hard to make sure our life as a family was good. When I say *good*, I don't mean by the standards of the world. For example, it was not unusual for the hot water to go out because we hadn't paid the bill, so Mom would boil water and pour it in the tub with cold water for us to bathe. Several times, when things got really bad, she took us to a fast-food restaurant to clean up in their bathroom. She found one with a drain in the middle of the bathroom floor. We stood over the drain, and she would pour water over our heads and wash us down, dry us off, dress us, and send us to school. There was one place close by our home where we could buy day-old doughnuts and get clean. We called it a truck stop for poor people. Sometimes Mom would knock on the back door of a place and ask if we could work for food. Many times our little family cleaned up a parking lot, took out trash, or cleaned tables in exchange for lunch or dinner.

When I started raising my children, we were really in trouble—no money at all. One day I struck up a conversation with a man in front of a car repair place outside Los Angeles, and he let me have a little car for fifty dollars. That was our home for quite a while.

I was never a person to say, "We don't have it." I'd say, "Let's go get it." One day we were in that little car and we saw a sign on the side of the road: "Painters Wanted."

I told the kids to hide in the bushes and I would get that job, even though I didn't know anything about painting. Well, I got it, and Charles, my oldest son, and I painted day and night, night and day until we got enough money to afford a little apartment.

LYNNE WILLIAMS, RON'S MOM

We moved a lot—all around Southern California. The bills would catch up with Mom, and *boom*, we would be off to the next place, moving just before she got the eviction notice. Even today my younger brother starts getting anxious if he's not packing for the next move.

We had second-hand furniture, and were thankful to get it. I remember the time my mother bought a white sofa from a second-hand furniture store, and I was so excited about that thing—literally elated. For several years we lived in a motor home, probably because it allowed us even looser ties. So we moved and moved and moved.

All this time, Mom dealt with four kids with all of our demands, getting us enrolled in school, trying to help us with homework. How do you get your arms around that? Not until much later did I realize the sleepless nights she must have endured as a mother. I'm sure there were times when she feared losing us because of her inability to take care of us financially.

The place I remember most fondly was the two-bedroom apartment in Ontario, California, in the midst of a twenty-acre complex, where my brothers and I played football in the grass under the trees, and I sat on the curb every day folding newspapers to deliver.

Ron learned at an early age that everybody working together could stave off a lot of bad things and add a lot of good things. He understands what it's like to be a part of a group. Scripture says three people bound together in a cord cannot be separated, and there were five us. We could not be separated, and we cannot be separated, no matter what.

LYNNE WILLIAMS, RON'S MOM

With four children in a two-bedroom apartment, my siblings and I all shared a room. If more than two of us were sharing the bed, we usually slept head to foot, and it wasn't unusual to wake up with somebody else's foot in your face.

Thank goodness for humor. We were a close family, and we laughed a lot. We're still very close.

At times Mom worked two jobs, and also did assembly work for two or three different marine crafting places at home at night and on weekends. She literally set up an assembly line in our living room, and we would assemble blocks for boat engines until bedtime. Mom would keep working long after we all went to bed, then she'd wake up exhausted, with nothing but dirty laundry in the house and no lunch money. There were times when she would tell us we had to stay home from school.

My brothers and sister would say, "Sweet!" and climb back into bed. But I had places I needed to go and people I needed to see, even as a kid. I needed to go to school. So I would hand-wash some clothes, blow-dry them, iron them, and walk to school. I'm sure Miss Frey had something to do with that.

THE GREATEST LESSON

Miss Frey was my fourth-grade teacher at Sultana Elementary School. More than anybody else in my life, she planted the idea of greatness in me.

In my elementary school days, and still today, fires burn in the mountains that rise east of the city. The school district held a contest among the eighteen elementary schools in our district to paint pictures of fire. The winner would receive a $100 savings bond.

─────────

My children never asked me for anything in the store. Not gum, or candy, or a quarter, or anything. We had an understanding that we got what we could.

LYNNE WILLIAMS, RON'S MOM

─────────

Now, I am not and never have been an artist, but Miss Frey encouraged me. So I ripped out a sheet of starch paper and painted something, and somehow I was selected to represent my school in the district contest. For the finals we went to the fire department, and there were seventeen beautiful pictures of fire lined up across the wall—and my ugly, ugly painting. Then the fire chief stood up and announced the third-place winner of a $25 savings bond, then the second-place winner. Then he announced the first-place winner—and he called my name. I looked around and asked, "What?" But Miss Frey was smiling and encouraging me to step forward and receive the prize.

It wasn't until years later when I was looking at a picture of that event—the fire chief shaking my hand and Miss Frey standing behind me—that I understood what had happened. My teacher had been my campaign manager—my greatest encourager. I have so much respect and gratitude for the difference she made in my life.

When I finished fourth grade, Miss Frey wrote an eight-page letter to me on beautiful blue stationery—an unbelievable note of love projecting onto me leadership, accomplishment, personality, music, sports, and the biggest world possible. I read that note day after day, especially when I was feeling uncertain or low, and I believed

—————————

I was sixteen when I had my first child. We all grew up together. We saw people hurting. We saw drugs and alcohol abuse. We saw people starving. We helped people, and people helped us. We learned what the world was about. If anyone in my home had five cents, it belonged to the house. Sometimes I needed money for dinner, and one day I said, "You guys, I need eleven dollars today." Well, my children hit the sidewalk and found pop bottles, swept porches for neighbors, took out trash, and mowed lawns. Pretty soon I heard them running up the alley yelling, "Mom! Mom!" They had the eleven dollars, and they had found other articles in the trash and brought them to me. Ron gave me a waffle iron, Eddie gave me a little half-full bottle of perfume, Chuck gave me a camera, and Sheryl gave me a little box of stationery and declared, "It's almost all here, Mommy!"

LYNNE WILLIAMS, RON'S MOM

—————————

every word of it. She played a huge role in my life, encouraging me to become anything I could dream. I'll never know whether she saw in me some special potential or she wrote letters like that to all her students. What I do know is that the belief she instilled in me changed my life.

A FINE BEAN

At Sultana Elementary School one year, we planted lima beans as a science experiment, then put our little cups of dirt and seed by the window to soak up sunshine. We had a four-day weekend coming up, and I couldn't bear to leave my little lima bean growing alone that whole time. So every day I walked over to the school and peeked into the window to see how my lima bean was doing.

I stared in at the cup with my name written on it and literally willed it to grow. "Come on, little bean," I said, "you can do it."

The next week we all went back to school, and I ran over to the table with the lima beans to see. Little plants had emerged in every cup—most of them a half-inch to an inch tall. But one of them was four and a half inches tall— the one growing out of the cup with my name on it. I was so awestruck I practically fell into my desk as I considered what had happened. To this day I don't know what made my little bean grow faster than the others. All I knew then was that my bean was going to grow in a great way, and I was committed and focused on it. Today I approach the domains in my life like the lima bean, knowing we can grow if we believe.

———————————

A lot of people can be the president or CEO of a company. A lot of people can pay attention to detail and do the company things. Not so many can empower people to do those things for the company. Ron brings a vision of enabling and empowerment to others; he thrusts that onto us so we can run with it and do the same with others.

DAYLEN BUSHMAN
VICE PRESIDENT OF MANUFACTURING AND FULFILLMENT

———————————

We had a stronghold in the Pacific Rim market at the company where I used to work. That went away about the time Ron came into the company. Ron had the opportunity to let some people go, but instead he kept us strong as a team. He was able to rally us and get us through tough times. We all became better people for that.

JERRY GRAY
SENIOR VICE PRESIDENT OF OPERATIONS
AND PRODUCT DEVELOPMENT

HARMONY

Harmony transforms a soul in seconds.

—

R.W.

I WAS a closet musician as a kid. I'd hear a song and sing it forty times before I went to bed. One year I asked Mom if I could have a guitar, knowing full well we couldn't afford it, but she supported me. I begged, borrowed, and worked for money until I had enough to buy that guitar, then I locked myself in the bedroom and taught myself to play "Tom Dooley," a folk song about a man condemned to hang. That was the beginning of my childhood dreams of "stardom."

Hang down your head, Tom Dooley
Hang down your head and cry
Hang down your head, Tom Dooley
Poor boy, you're bound to die

Over time I learned to play the piano and drums, and I started writing music with a passion. My brother and I were in the Claremont Boys Choir, and we both won a scholarship for six months at a music school in England. Mom really wanted us to go, but we knew if we did, we'd lose our paper routes—we both had more than two hundred customers—so we stayed home. Years later I had the opportunity to sing with some big-name people, even touring and singing duets with Marie Osmond. It became clear, though, that my career was the musical equivalent of an artist relegated to sketching caricatures at the carnival— singing backup on somebody else's stage. So I put that aside as a career and allowed music to become a passion.

Looking back on the lessons I learned from music, I see that it taught me the discipline of practice, development, harmony, and listening, all of which have been important to my success in business.

BAD CHOICES, GOOD CHOICES

Growing up I saw people make choices that left them barely getting by financially, or they made personal health choices like smoking that I knew would have a negative impact. I can't point to a day and a time, but somewhere along the way I made a choice—I decided to use my time to pursue something better, whether it was music, sports, or simply choosing friends. I was attracted to people who had good things going on, and even though I was usually the only guy in the mix who didn't have anything, I was sitting at the table with people who had stuff. Sometimes I didn't feel worthy of being there—like I was just a fly on the wall watching what was going on. But for some reason—maybe my friends understood at some level my innermost thoughts, and that was more important to them than outward appearances—people projected leadership or success onto me that initially I didn't see in myself.

———————————

Harmony is the ability to differ. Look at light, how the beautiful, varied colors of the rainbow come together. Are you aware of the importance of harmony?

When my family was all together pulling in harmony, we created miracles. When we were disruptive with each other and going in different directions, I could see our family falling apart, and it crushed my insides. Whenever I see loneliness, it hurts me.

Today I work with beautiful people of different races, age, and gender, and just like my family when I was growing up, I see how powerful we can be together. Of course, there are times when we get sidetracked, and I see us get off track. Just like when I was a child, that hurts me deep inside.

But this industry can bring us together from around the world in a profound way if we will allow it, as long as we don't approach things with a "do me" or "taker's" mentality. That only creates greed and isolation. When we come together with a vision bigger than all of us so none of us can get in the way, that is network marketing at its best.

R.W.

My Introduction
to Network Marketing

There were only a few times during my growing-up years when I was embarrassed by how little our family had. But then I went to college, and my classmates drove up in the new cars their parents had given them for high school graduation, and I began to realize how different my childhood had been.

I also came to understand that nothing is wrong with having nice things. But when nice things—what you drive or what you wear—become your identity, that's a problem. I don't want to chase the next toy. I want to chase the next opportunity to give or share or sacrifice.

I wasn't good in college at all, though I saw the value in learning and socializing—I majored in people. My plan was to become a broadcast journalist specializing in advertising and marketing.

During college I was introduced to the company NuSkin, a "network marketing" company. Well, I thought network marketing had something to do with computers. When I learned they were doing facials, I said naively, "I'm going to college to get a *real* job."

Ron has always been kind, and somewhat accident-prone. He was trying to help a neighbor cut his lawn, and he spilled some gasoline onto his sock. About that time another neighbor threw a lit cigarette in his direction, and it ignited his feet. His brother, Charles, saw what was happening and tackled him to put his feet out. They both got burned. Yes, Ron is accident-prone, but very caring.

LYNNE WILLIAMS, RON'S MOM

———————————

Many people will go to college and spend thousands of dollars and borrow thousands more to earn their certification to be a dental hygienist or an accountant or a lawyer. Then they graduate and realize nothing has changed *who* they are becoming—only *what* they are becoming.

R.W.

———————————

Before long, though, I became a NuSkin distributor; then I grew into an opportunity to work closely with the founders of the company, where I saw how the connections worked and how people were making a lot of money.

NuSkin was my first introduction to real corporate America, and my friends made bets I wouldn't last a month in a corporate environment. They thought I was too free-spirited to make it with a corporation.

In my first meeting with the top executives, we were brainstorming, and I came up with thirteen ideas. They liked what I had said and asked, "Send us all a memo to recap your thoughts."

"Absolutely," I responded.

Well, I thought a memo was what your mom put on the fridge to remind you to do your chores; that's how naive I was. So I wrote my ideas on thirteen sticky notes, one for each idea, and stuck them to their doors. The next day they were laughing and saying, "And he's funny too!" They didn't know I was serious. That was my introduction to the corporate world. I was, and am, what you might call a barefoot white-collar guy. I can wear a suit and play the corporate game, but I have to keep it grounded and keep it real.

Many of us have worked with other network marketing companies where management had an adversarial relationship with their distributors and did not care about the nature of a product as long as it was selling. Ron inverted that relationship. The primary reason we exist as a company is to help people build businesses to be successful. To do that, we provide high-quality products that improve health just by adding them to your daily regimen.

TIM SIMPSON, CHIEF INFORMATION OFFICER

Other companies where I worked were more political. The sales team might not like the marketing team, and they kept secrets from each other. Accounting was always the enemy—the "no" group because they always said no. The open environment here gives everybody a chance to express his or her opinion and make a difference.

ROBERT REITZ
SENIOR VICE PRESIDENT OF BUSINESS ANALYSIS

PEOPLE FIRST

*I never want to find myself at the top of some mountain,
lonely with a bag of money*

—

R. W.

A SUBSEQUENT opportunity at another network marketing company, Neways, allowed me to work around the world, learning other cultures and ways of living. Through that experience I learned that we can't sit here in our little offices in Utah and make livelihood decisions for people who are on the other side of the world. Too many companies sit in their little bubbles and make life-changing decisions for other people while they're sleeping. Instead, we should be engaging them, learning their culture, mind-set, economy, and competition, then tuning into that and getting busy.

I was working with Neways when the Mexican peso was devalued by more than half, in comparison with the U.S. dollar. Our contracts had been written in a way that did not take into account devaluation of the currency, and the company was about to start losing a lot of money. So they sent me down there to close our operation.

I went to Mexico City for the first time on that trip, and I was scared to death. Then as soon as I met the people, I fell in love with them. They all lived in the moment and wore their hearts on their sleeves and in service to their fellowman.

Most Americans, I soon learned, saw this servant mentality through the lens of their own "superiority." But the Mexican people didn't see it that way. They were authentically loving, serving, and open—not guarded, jaded, and filtering. I fell in love with them and wanted to live there. There was no way I could shut down the operation.

So counter to what I had been sent to do, I went to UPS, the local landlords for the office and the warehouse, and others and renegotiated all the contracts. Then I renegotiated all the salaries of the local staff.

By that time, the company had stopped sending product to Mexico; so the sales force had nothing to sell. So we created a simple, practical path to economic success by selling toilet paper—nothing but toilet paper, tissue, and napkins. We had a personal development card and tape that said, in essence, "Hang in there. This is when giants and leaders emerge."

For months we sold toilet paper in big black plastic bags—more toilet paper than any network marketing company in the history of man.

Because we were absolutely committed to weathering that crisis, not only did we maintain the company but also grew it. Then we renegotiated all the contracts with the company and reintroduced its products, allowing the Mexico team to grow to a multimillion-dollar monthly revenue.

NEW DAD, NEW PERSPECTIVE

By now I was married, and our daughter, Maron, had been born. But within months of her birth, my wife decided that being a mother wasn't for her.

Every day of my life as a father I have thought about my own mother and tried to follow her model, even

———————

I was working for Neways in 1994 and we had just begun our operations in Mexico when our government devalued the currency overnight. It was the worst economic crisis ever in Mexico, and we've had some bad ones. We got word that the company was sending Mr. Ron Williams to help us. I prepared to meet this man, expecting him to be a big executive type—a short, fat, older guy with gray hair or maybe bald. So this young guy walks in wearing shorts and a jersey and a cap on backward, and I ask, "Where's Mr. Ron Williams?" Boy, was I surprised!

Ron was a cool guy, and so young for such an important position, vice president of sales.

He met with all of our employees and

many of our distributors, and he immediately connected with us. He understood how we had put our hopes and dreams into that business.

Then he told us that he had been sent to Mexico to shut down the operation, but he believed he could avoid that. What was at stake then was real people, real lives, real families. He made it clear that his priority was our people first, and he took a stand for us. He made commitments to us, and he met those commitments. He earned all my respect.

Mexico grew so strong for the company that we became the support for starting operations in other countries. That wouldn't have happened if Ron had taken the easy way.

JORGE E. ALVARADO
VICE PRESIDENT OF LATIN AMERICAN BUSINESS DEVELOPMENT

though my life as a single parent was much different from hers. Most mornings I brought my daughter to work with me in her little car seat, where she sat on my desk. I rocked her, fed her, changed her diapers in the men's room down the hall. Seeing her all day, every day, grounded me and reminded me, "You are committed, Ron, committed to your profession and to people. You are responsible."

Had Maron not been there, it would have been easy for me to walk out of my life and my career. Instead, she served as an inspiration to me, an inspiration for my success. Her presence in my life encouraged me to reach beyond my career and our little family and to take a stand in the world. And that has made all the difference.

While I was growing professionally, the leadership at Neways demonstrated their commitment to the whole person, not just the business aspect of their employees. They were completely cool with my bringing Maron to work with me. I'll always be grateful to them for letting me grow—as a father and a professional at the same time.

After nearly seven years I had worked my way to the top at Neways, but I felt I hadn't reached my potential. Money didn't have a lot of meaning for me, and I couldn't see that I was growing in any other way. So with no plan for my future except to seek a new way to grow, and with the belief that I had developed the skills to figure out what was next, I gave a two-week notice and walked out. My peers thought I was crazy.

PATIENCE

One of the hardest things I've had to learn in a corporate environment is patience. I'm a forward thinker; I see cause and effect.

Years ago I was working in a corporate environment, and a lot of the office politics made no sense. I know now that certain actions arose from people simply trying to coexist in a big office. Still, there were days when I felt completely lifeless.

The day I reached my limit in that company, and could no longer stomach the silly games, I was getting ready to walk out the door. I didn't know, of course, that I was right in the middle of the bridge to an understanding of leadership, and if I had walked away from the industry that day, I probably never would have returned. All I knew was that I couldn't take any more corporate politics.

———————————

As a young, single dad, I was often awkward when it came to picking out my daughter's clothes or fixing her hair. Everybody knows I have those days when my taste in clothes and design turns awful. But the joy she has brought into my life transcends all of those outward kinds of things.

Maron will wake up in the morning, and the first thing she does is smile. Sometimes when I wake up early and I'm having a bad morning, I'll selfishly wake her up just to see her smile.

She gets out of bed and immediately looks through the blinds at the sky to measure the blue-sky-to-cloud ratio.

One day we were driving in traffic, and I was irritable.

"I love traffic," Maron said.

"Why?" I asked.

"Because everybody becomes so peaceful."

And instantly, I became more peaceful. What she was seeing was everybody slowing down for each other—merging and taking turns.

On Halloween a few years ago we saw searchlights, and she said, "Dad, God is looking for somebody."

She saw the searchlights as pointing down.

I think you can understand how she is my inspiration.

R.W.

That very day I picked up a magazine with an article about how to work successfully in a corporation. The author suggested that instead of giving all your energy to the things going on at the sidelines—in sports analogy, instead of going up to the skybox and looking at everything happening on the field—go onto the field and play. Sweat, bleed, and work with the team. That is the measure of character.

The magazine said if you will kick butt today and let go of all the sideline issues, politics, and stories, then tomorrow will take care of itself.

From that day forward I chose to get lost in each day and make as much happen as I could right then, so that my future would always be in my control.

That was the breakthrough in my career that allowed me to stay in the ring every day and let tomorrow take care of itself.

THE LIFEBLOOD OF PLANTS

What came next was Young Living Essential Oils. I didn't even know what essential oils were; I thought you had to live in Sedona, Arizona, to understand how they worked.

Immediately, though, I fell in love with essential oils, which are nothing more than the lifeblood of plants, the oldest medicine known to man, more precious than gold and silver for thousands of years. I would have stayed at that company forever but for one person with power who was not living his truths. I learned that on a Wednesday night and resigned on Thursday morning. It was serious.

Money is neutral, neither good nor bad. It can make good people better and bad people worse.

R.W.

I knew then that it was time to start my own company—Whole Living, majoring in whole foods. People are sick and tired of taking a bottle of capsules that are supposed to be miracle pills to change your life and give you an excuse to live an unhealthy lifestyle. I think that's how we got into our current unhealthy mess, especially in this country. Whole Living, which became Brain Garden, specialized in organic,

Going to Maron's first-grade Christmas concert became one of the most heart-wrenching lessons in parenting I would ever experience. I fell short so badly. Her teacher had sent home the songs for her to learn, and we didn't take time to practice them or anything.

We arrived at the concert, and I found a seat. Soon Maron's class came out, and there she was, in the center of the front row. I smiled and caught her eye, and she smiled back. Then they started singing, and Maron didn't know the lyrics. As her classmates smiled and sang, Maron began to cry in her embarrassment. As her dad, I just wanted to disappear—to scoop her up and land someplace, anyplace else.

Afterward I held her hand as we walked out to the parking lot, and I made a commitment to myself and to her to take greater responsibility—not to rely on and expect others to do those things she needed from her dad.

The saying is true; it takes a village to raise a child. But first, it takes parents who commit.

R.W.

———————————

clean, whole foods, and it was euphoric at its height. As we quickly grew, we decided to take the company public before we had a good understanding of how a public company worked. We brought on new people to help us through all of that, but this created so much conflict we lost our message. Heartbroken, I had to go to our shareholders and say, in effect, "I'm not putting myself in a position where I have to sit on a witness stand beside either one of those guys."

So I resigned with a lot of stock and a lot of money and went into retirement. I bought a house and a Harley and grew lazier by the day. My life was so quiet, I started checking the telephone for a dial tone.

Then one day—it was the middle of the afternoon—I was sitting on the sofa in my pajamas watching Oprah Winfrey cry. I knew then that I had to do something with my life. I had become one of the people I had seen for so long—building out the extremities of my life, thinking the toys would fulfill me. They didn't. In fact, without personal growth, the more you build on the extremities, the emptier you feel.

I knew I had to work on myself.

LOOKING FOR MORE
THAN "RAH RAH!"

My impression of personal development courses was somebody standing in front of the room going *rah rah rah*, and at the back of the room assistants getting ready to close the deal on books and tapes. I knew I needed guidance, but I resisted those courses. I didn't see value in spending thousands of dollars, even going into debt, for some education curriculum certificate. Most of the courses, it seemed, were about becoming somebody, when, in fact, becoming somebody is not *what* you are but *who* you are.

Then I heard about a course that was amazingly creative and experiential. I joined forty other people from many states, all of us bringing widely differing backgrounds. There were successful professionals, housewives, and several who were unemployed. I was so turned inside out and so optimistic about life, I took the challenge to look beyond myself.

After completing the course, I drove across the valley to the apartment complex where I had lived my most formative childhood years. There, sitting on the curbside where I had folded thousands of newspapers, in front of the little apartment where I grew up, I reflected on where I had come from and where I was at that moment. I watched the children play under the same trees I played under three decades earlier. Recalling my mother's strength, I felt a renewed gratitude for my childhood, our struggles, and the woman who poured so much love and energy into raising her children.

I was, and am, grateful for my roots. That experience is part of who I am—a rounding off of my character. I am living proof that it doesn't matter where you come from economically. That is my mother's gift to me and my siblings.

Some children, whether they are raised in poverty or with a silver spoon, grow to resent family, siblings, and money, or the lack of it. To the contrary, I'm thankful this is where I started. The only bit of sadness I feel is knowing that my mom lived through her early twenties with four children and no family nearby to help. I have no idea how she held it together. It's a pleasure now to be able to take care of my mother and repay her for sacrifices she made for us.

As I sat there on the curb, I thought about the nearly fifty thousand people who would join the network marketing industry that very day, along with nearly fifty thousand more the next day and the next. *What if,* I thought, *we could*

Ron genuinely wants to see the world become a global community of givers. That's his vision for the world, for network marketing, for his life, and for the lives of people he cares about. A lot of people have big dreams and don't believe they can come true. Ron believes his dream will come true. Every day he moves toward his vision. Being president of MLMIA [Multi-Level Marketing International Association] is not just a title or an opportunity to go to more conventions. He has a vision for this industry to take a stand and get everybody on board.

ALLISON KING, EXECUTIVE ASSISTANT

change the industry into a community of givers—people who want to touch the world and make a difference in it?

Some in the network marketing industry, like many the world around us, begin by saying, "Do me." They begin the conversation by asking, "What's your product? What's your comp plan? What's your product? What's your comp plan?" If the company wins financially, they win, but if the company loses, its distributors lose. They don't want to put any skin in the game.

I didn't want any part of that. I knew that we could build a business with purpose and meaning and passion— a business that would make a real difference in the world. Too many of us think the world is some intangible thing out there that we can't touch or change, when in reality it is always right here, right now, all the time. Because of the degrees of separation, you and I know everybody in the world. We are absolutely linked. Every decision we make should reflect that understanding.

I thought about how far I had come in my life, and yet it paled in comparison to what my mother had done bringing up four children with the financial challenges she faced. I declared that day to start a company with a vision and purpose bigger than all of us, so that we couldn't get in the way,

Money is not my only motivation. I am motivated equally by purpose and a cause. I have learned that money is an important component to creating these things, and a lot of good things can be done with money.

R.W.

yet with the right business fundamentals to catapult us financially and allow us to achieve that vision. At the same time I felt a burning desire to reach out to more than just the people who are on the same lane in life I'm on. I saw the potential of connecting all of humanity and knew that would be a profound thing to do in business. I knew I would be passionate and my will would be iron if I aligned with something where there was nothing in it for me—if I would focus on helping others and empowering others to better themselves. Not just saying it from the stage, but being it. Embodying it.

Once more I thought of Mom, and I wondered what would happen if CEOs were more like mothers. Mothers are esteemed as the core of love around our world—the nurturing, healing, loving side of humanity. If we take that idea into business, then CEOs are in essence the mothers of the business world if they choose to accept that role. They can make a profound difference in the world if they become conscious of everything and everyone around them.

In that moment, I made the determination that I would start a business and do something with purpose and meaning, with the full intention of giving back.

You have the same choice. You can talk about the bigger picture, humanity, and corporate responsibility, or you can say, "Hey, look, I'm running a business. Isn't that enough?"

It absolutely is not. It's the vision that brings hope during challenging times. If you can run a business, you can influence humanity. The person running the business has an influence in the community. But business can show gratitude too. If you're doing everything for the bottom line, what are you doing for the community?

So when do you start? Are you going to take, take, take, and then when you get enough, start giving back? How much is enough? When do you shift gears from taking to giving?

Look at your priorities *now*. You can help make your community better today and also run your business. In fact, the two go hand-in-hand.

If you can enhance the belief system in humankind by creating an experience for your customers and your employees that goes above and beyond fundamental business, that's what it's all about.

Our challenge is to find that balance between aggressiveness in business and service to the community. We never want to trade one for the other. We can still be wildly successful and maintain our principles.

Ron trusts with high expectations. I'll get a three- or four-word voice mail, and then he gives me freedom to do the job. He trusts. He doesn't watch. Later, if we're not aligned on it, we'll talk about it.

CRAIG SMITH, DIRECTOR OF COMMUNITY STANDS

ForeverGreen is my home. It's my family. Even when times are tough or we have difficult things we need to work through together, they're always there, always loving.

ALLISON KING, EXECUTIVE ASSISTANT

A WAY OF BEING

To achieve something you first need to be something.
Otherwise, it's all just fake.

—

JORGE E. ALVARADO
Vice President of Latin American Business Development

WHEN I decided on the name ForeverGreen for the
new company, I went to an art gallery and asked the
artist, Jon McNaughton, to create four paintings of the
same landscape, but to show it in all four seasons. He
looked at me like was I was crazy, and must have been
wondering how I would pay for his work. (I was dressed
in sweats with my visor on backward and probably some

spaghetti sauce on my shirt.) We talked for a while about the vision of ForeverGreen, and when I explained that I wanted an evergreen tree in the top right corner of each painting, I saw the light come on. He got it.

When seasons change, the evergreen embraces every second of every season of its life. It's always green, always growing, no matter the conditions around it.

How many of us embrace every season of our life? How many of us understand that today's ceiling is tomorrow's ground floor?

Often we gravitate to what feels comfortable to us rather than embracing the cold weather. When we embrace the cold, it will form our character, and we can move on to the next season. When we resist, Groundhog Day continues in our life. The same things happen again and again until we step through it. ForeverGreen is the epitome of stepping through it.

ForeverGreen isn't a product; it's a way of being. Whether we are young, middle-age, or old, we embrace every second of every season of our lives.

The one piece of advice I remember my father giving me was when I was really young and playing baseball. He said, "When you get up to the plate, swing the bat as hard as you can, because you might just hit the ball."

That's the way I try to live every part of my life, always swinging for the fences.

R.W.

A BIG VISION

One reason ForeverGreen's vision is so big is because when we started, we had no product. I had signed a noncompete agreement when I left Brain Garden, so at least in the beginning I knew we would be extremely limited in the products we could introduce. Instead of developing a broad product line, we focused on the impact we could make in the world. We also made sure we had the right people.

Because we based ForeverGreen on timeless principles, and because we built it on truth, there is a congruency between the people who work here, the products we market, and the literature we write. I look at the people who have joined our corporate side who are beautiful people from top to bottom, and I don't think that's an accident. I see people who have come in and started their home-based businesses who are beautiful, who have made our vision bigger, better, and more tangible, and I don't think that's an accident. I do believe there is a correlation between the top and bottom, and that works for good or bad. ForeverGreen is true. It's good. ForeverGreen feels right. Energy does not lie. At its core, ForeverGreen is a beautiful thing. Occasionally, we have

―――――――――――

Self-consumption—"Do me"—leads to isolation, alienation, and depression. That doesn't work in life. The whole idea of ForeverGreen is to realize the world isn't "out there." It's not some intangible thing we can't touch. It's something here and now, inside us. It's always here, always now. We can touch the world every single day. That is an empowering, contagious notion. Wherever you're at and with whomever you are with at the moment.

R.W.

―――――――――――

people who show up and say, "Do me," and I say, "You have the wrong company." ForeverGreen is about making all of us better.

Ray Kinsella in *Field of Dreams* knew that if he built it, they would come. We started ForeverGreen believing that our message and our purpose would attract good people.

For example, I had a group of friends who were quite successful at another network marketing company, and I refrained from telling them the ForeverGreen message for fear I might take their passion for what they were doing.

Finally I told them and, bless their hearts, they made a leap of faith from that great income and jumped to ForeverGreen—before we had our first product! They became some of our first distributors and have helped build the foundation of our company.

None of them had any idea what our products would be. They only knew that we had a big mission and purpose greater than all of us. They made a huge statement of leadership and trust in us by coming on board at such an early time, despite the unknown.

At the same time, we obviously needed at least a single product to sell. I started looking into chocolate, which we were not prohibited from selling by my noncompete

I was at the decision point of leaving the industry, frustrated and unable to see the good it could do. Then Ron Williams came as a consultant to the company where I was working and he told us about a vision for a higher purpose, of people who could change lives, and I believed him. His message confirmed for me that there is good in our industry.

BEN ALLEN, DIRECTOR OF MARKETING

agreement, and in my research I learned that chocolate is the number-one craved food in the world. It's actually the seed of a fruit—an extension of the grocery store produce section. The problem with most chocolate, I learned, is the addition of refined sugar, wax, hormone-treated dairy, flavorings, preservatives, and all kinds of other things in the name of commercialization. That's why so many people associate chocolate with guilt.

In reality, chocolate is a natural, healthy, whole food that is the number-one antioxidant in the food chain. In its raw form, it is a beautiful thing. Chocolate is great for the circulation. It makes you feel good, and it makes you happy.

We began looking for the right chocolate product that aligned with our vision, and we found 24 Karat Chocolate bars—pure, organic dark chocolate in its most natural form, with no added flavorings. I was amazed at how good it tasted.

We created 24 Karat Teasers and used them as a door-opener to tell people about our vision. We were off and running.

———————————

In the beginning it seemed crazy—start a health company with chocolate? I had some concerns there. Then I saw the facts, especially that chocolate is extremely high in antioxidants, and I thought, Why not? If you can make a healthy choice with the highest-quality organic chocolate, that can work. It was a lot of fun, even frantic at times, with a down-home, everybody-is-family feel to the office as we brought 24 Karat Chocolate to the market.

BEN ALLEN, DIRECTOR OF MARKETING

———————————

ALIGNMENT

Alignment supersedes mechanism. That means each of us must be open to communicating across functions within the corporation, up and down the ranks, from the corporate office to the individual distributor, to ensure that the corporate office is working in the best interest of each individual and for the greater good.

Here's a story to explain how alignment works: Suppose you and I are business partners with another friend—we'll call her Brenda—and we want to do something to help tsunami victims, who need food, shelter, money, resources, medical treatment, and education. We're looking for a way to generate the resources to help, and I remember that my neighbor makes umbrellas. "I think we can get them for three dollars and sell them for twenty bucks," I tell you and Brenda, as I try to align you with my idea.

Then Brenda says, "I think we can all sell chocolate and generate even more money."

You speak up next and say, "I have a contact in Brazil who makes toothpicks out of recycled wood. We can get several toothpicks for a penny. Every household needs a box, and every restaurant needs a case."

You totally enroll us, and we decide to align with you on toothpicks.

What we need to understand here is that the mechanism—toothpicks, chocolate, or umbrellas—isn't as important as our alignment. We were already aligned in our desire to help tsunami victims. Once we truly align with toothpicks, we'll sell more toothpicks than any three people in all of history, and then we can serve the greater purpose—helping tsunami victims.

Too often in corporations, people walk out of a meeting grumbling, "I told them chocolate would sell more," or "I can't believe they didn't go with umbrellas."

The point is, we could have sold umbrellas, chocolate, or toothpicks. As long as we are objective and honest with each other and look to align, we will succeed together. But if you're not in alignment, you're in the way.

—————————————

What sets a company apart in this industry is the vision of that company—to be able to link as many people in the world to see the same vision and achieve a goal together. Our community stand connects people of every race and every culture. Having a community stand allows us to fulfill our natural desire to better our lives and other people's lives. We're not just a product company, and we're not just a comp plan company. By giving, we have the best of both, and at the same time we have an even bigger vision.

BRENDA HUANG, CHIEF MARKETING OFFICER

—————————————

Health, kindness, and opportunity are not just words. They form the foundational questions we ask ourselves whenever we are undertaking projects or making decisions about the way we operate.

TIM SIMPSON, CHIEF INFORMATION OFFICER

HEALTH

Look around and see how any people have visions of love, spirituality, and family for their lives. Health is the connector to all these things.

—

R.W.

PEOPLE OFTEN ask me, "What does health have to do with the ForeverGreen message?"

"Everything," I say. "Health is my biggest passion."

The message of ForeverGreen is that whether we are young, middle-age, or old, we must embrace every second of life in every season. Health is the connecter that allows us to embrace life.

The four paintings on the cover of this book, the ones I commissioned as we were creating ForeverGreen, may help you understand that concept. The first painting is of fall, when everything is dying and shedding its skin. Yet there stands the evergreen tree, bright radiant green, much like the girl or boy you once were. "I am a sponge," you said. "Teach me. Show me." While all around you was changing, you never doubted that you could be anything you wanted when you grew up—doctor or nurse, fireman or policeman, even president. And you were kind to everyone.

The season changes to winter, and the evergreen still glows bright green in the dramatically changed surroundings. In fact, it has grown. My interpretation of this painting is that the tree now represents a teenager, growing physically while experiencing new emotional depth and power, rejection and confidence, and self-esteem. For the first time the tree feels the cold chills of life's challenges and is ready to become an adult.

Then we enter the spring of our lives, and hope is in the air. We are young adults, full of life and health—feeling invincible. We have so much energy and so much life to live. In fact, we're so strong we can carry others on our shoulders. We fall in love. We realize that this is what health and well-being feels like.

Summer comes and everything is in full bloom. We should have it all. Yet this is the time when many of us surrender to fear, choosing to be a survivor with little hope. We pull back and withdraw just when we should be doing our best. Shouldn't life get better with age? Look around! Like the evergreen tree in summer, we are surrounded with abundance and joy. Live and grow into that abundance and enjoy!

I live in a cabin by a stream in the mountains, where I see nature continually reinventing itself. In the fall I watch the trees release their leaves—shedding themselves to go into winter and recreate themselves again.

Sometimes life comes at you from all directions. We look around and see how many people doubt their ability to recreate life and sustain their dreams. I ask, "Who created the life you have?" When you realize you are the author of the life you have, you can create whatever you want to do. You can live a life by design or by default. It's your choice.

STANDING IN THE DRIFT

The earth is in constant transformation, always recreating itself to be an abundant resource. As earth's seasons change, so do conditions around us—health, finances, relationships. Like the evergreen tree, we grow by embracing these conditions and stepping through our fears to stand in the drift.

The drift is like a raging river. Turn on the news or read the paper, and you see war, hunger, hatred, greed. Some people in business will do anything to get to the top.

When we take a stand, we become like a rock in that torrent that rushes past us. While it's not a mandate, ForeverGreen is a large body of people doing small, random acts of kindness that make a big difference in the world today. Just ten minutes a day or ten hours a month in soup kitchens, orphanages, convalescence homes, abuse shelters, or on environmental and wildlife issues. It can even be helping a neighbor. We get outside ourselves long enough to make someone else happy and to make a difference. Since the day we opened for business, at our corporate office we have given all our employees an extended lunch one day a month and encouraged them to serve completely outside themselves giving back to the community.

We call it "taking a stand," because no matter what is rushing by us in the river of this changing world, we are

Ron truly lives his compassion on an employee level at ForeverGreen as well as with family and in the community. Even his business ventures are about compassion. He truly lives his community stand every day, being compassionate to others.

ALLISON KING, EXECUTIVE ASSISTANT

choosing to stand firm, and that choice literally changes our lives.

Every year we begin our annual convention by taking a stand. Our distributors arrive at the convention, and we have twenty buses lined up to take them out into the community to serve. They can choose to help clean up a park or plant trees there, serve in an elderly care facility or a soup kitchen, or work with underprivileged children—any number of possibilities.

After doing that all day, we come back to opening night at the convention with a real spirit of giving. I believe the days are over when a CEO announces to the crowd, "We gave 2 percent to the rain forest," and everybody getting goose bumps are over. That's disempowering. It's the Superman syndrome, and it encourages people to say, "I gave at the office," so they can "give" without actually doing anything. Today it's about your hands and mine. It's about reaching out and touching the world.

ForeverGreen distributors take a community stand, something completely outside themselves, and it changes everything. A distributor has a rough day or a rough week, and he or she calls me with the news. I like to respond by asking, "What's your community stand?"

The impact of ForeverGreen can be measured person by person—not based on numbers but on actions. Thousands of people are doing random acts of kindness every day for people they don't even know.

JORGE E. ALVARADO
VICE PRESIDENT OF LATIN AMERICAN BUSINESS DEVELOPMENT

"I serve in a group home," the distributor might answer.

Then I say, "Well, go on out to that group home and call me back in an hour."

When they call back, instead of a long conversation about a product or a compensation plan, we talk about making a difference in the world. When you get involved in that, everything else seems pretty small.

Standing in the drift, we have learned, is the beginning of good mental, physical, and emotional health. In fact, kindness, health, and well-being go hand-in-hand, as small acts of kindness generate energy, stamina, and hope. Our bodies also have physical needs that must be met. We are, after all, electrical beings, so everything we put into our bodies should enhance our natural conductivity. You've heard the clichés: "I'm sick and tired of being sick and tired," or "You don't value health until you lose it." To create a better tomorrow, we must be responsible today.

A MULTIVITAMIN IN A BIG MAC

I look around and see how many people have visions of love or intimacy, spirituality, family, or money, but they are stepping over their health to get there, only to come up short. As a sick and overweight generation, we are raising the sickest generation of Americans ever and the fattest generation of Americans ever. We will become the first generation to outlive our kids. I refuse to be a part of that army of people who feel hopeless, cynical, and fearful.

Here we are in this fast-food world, this "Lunchables" era, with prescriptions to ease our pain and boy bands to entertain us, and our children think they're health nuts when it says "10 percent juice" on their candy. We eat foodless foods and drink lifeless drinks. Our children think eating fruit means eating *Fruit* Loops, *Apple* Jacks, and Crunch*berries*. Brightly colored packages depict beautiful pictures of food, but there's no food in it. Then they go to school and get a cheeseburger, fries, and a soda. And if they're "lucky" their parents order a pizza that night. There's no life in that. None. They've made no deposits into the account, just withdrawals. The food they've eaten sucks life and energy from the body just to process all those chemicals. And here are the results: the number-one killer of children by disease is cancer. Diabetes among children has quadrupled since the 1970s and will triple again in the next twenty years. For the first time in history, the number of overweight people rivals normal weight people—even among children. Heart

———————————

The one word that truly defines what is different about ForeverGreen is *heart*. Everybody involved in offices or in the field is engaged emotionally and intellectually. It's not just random things happening. People are looking to make a better life for themselves, and by extension, helping others have a better life as well.

TIM SIMPSON, CHIEF INFORMATION OFFICER

———————————

disease remains the number-one killer by disease in America.

The drift grows stronger as we get weaker. Synthetic chemicals and extended shelf lives are killing us and sending us downstream, and the only positive is we'll look a lot younger long after we die.

We can't step over the fundamentals to capture a vision. We must allow the fundamentals to catapult us to that place where we can live our vision. Health is the facilitator of all our dreams—the supreme law that connects us to those channels of spirituality and success in every other area of our life.

What's beautiful about nature is that it was designed for us long before we got here.

R.W

Health truly is the platform. That platform is built on nutrition, and there are no shortcuts.

Too many people today put a multivitamin in their Big Mac just to compensate for bad choices in their lives. They think that's what works. But that's what led us into this mess. Health and nutrition are about leveraging the magic bullet, and the magic bullet is your body, not a pill.

THE BEAUTY OF WHOLE FOODS

Nutrition was meant to be pleasurable. It always has been. Indigenous cultures didn't have road rage in the drive-through of a peach tree. They just picked it and ate it—the original fast food. They didn't have infomercials and billboards and pop-ups. They had the wind and the trees and their voices. They enjoyed whole foods and understood the link between whole foods and health long before science did. How right they were!

Today health has become a game of roulette. Truthful answers are slipping from our grasp, motivated by quick and easy commercialized "strategies." Disease has become the big mystery, and we nobly praise those who join forces to fight it. Billions of dollars are raised to fund the fight and create weapons of war: more high-priced patents for more high-priced drugs. These weapons in many cases have become friendly fire. Properly prescribed medications are among the top-ten killers in the United States. Listen closely to the next commercial you hear for a prescription drug, and you'll realize that the side effects can be worse than the disease itself.

Here are the words I want to hear: "Side effects may include energy, stamina, joy, and a better health sense of well-being."

Health is not an event. Health is a way of life, built on good choices that lead to good habits. It's the small things we do day after day that equate to wellness or diseases.

R.W.

At ForeverGreen we embrace all healers and doctors. You should know who to go to for what and when. We also believe, however, that your body is the greatest healer of all. Your body will perform miracles by the minute when you take responsibility by honoring the intelligence of the human body. First you have to give it the raw material. ForeverGreen has mastered the art of raw materials; we give you the finest raw materials in the world.

The truth is, health is simple. It's been around forever. It's also important to remember that health is a habit, not an event. The small decisions we make day after day ultimately determine our health and well-being.

Whoever said nutrition had to be a handful of pills and a frothy green drink on a Saturday? That's not health! You don't have to hold your nose and drink something to be healthy. In fact, there's nothing healthy about that.

At ForeverGreen we specialize in organic whole foods. A lot of people want to say, "We've found the answer at elevation 4000, and we extracted from the plant." Well, elevation 4000 might be fine, but don't extract from the plant. Take the plant in its whole form, because it's made up of thousands of phytonutrients that work like an army by land, by sea, and by air. They're supposed to work in the body together, so don't extract them. As soon as you extract it, you may have a super-concentration of one ingredient from that plant, but you've blown it. Don't rely on science and technology to manufacture the secret to good health. Find the secret in natural, whole foods. Nature in its whole form is nutritionally complex, so we don't have to be, and it offers the most effective way to achieve good health.

If you have traveled to Europe or Latin America, you surely have seen the *farmacia*. The Spanish spelling makes sense, because originally going to the "pharmacy" meant going to the farm—out to the garden and picking fruits, vegetables, herbs, and spices, and just eating them. Food was medicine; medicine was food. Then the farm was replaced by pharmacology, which is the study of toxicology, or how poisons work in your body. Now that industry names new diseases just so they can fuel the economic channel by offering a prescription to treat these new diseases.

The right idea, the whole idea, is that if God made it, eat it. If man made it, leave it alone or eat it in moderation. It's as simple as that.

SEVEN PRINCIPLES OF HEALTH

Timeless principles of health begin when we realize we are electrical beings. Our frequency has been measured at 40 mHz to 60 mHz. That's your life force, and you are to hunt for electricity from the moment you wake up until you go to bed. Imagine your energy as a bank account, and everything you put in your mouth or on your skin is either a deposit or a withdrawal. Fresh fruits like apples, and especially lemons, make deposits. In terms of frequency, lemons are the highest among foods. I plugged an electric clock into a lemon, and it ran for a month. Roses have the highest electrical frequency in the plant kingdom, and essential oils also have extremely high frequencies. (Wait until you hear about marine phytoplankton.)

On the other hand, foodless foods and lifeless drinks have low frequency and no power. When you put them into your body, you may think you're making a deposit, but you're actually making a withdrawal. They suck energy out of you.

The following principles of health allow us to continually make deposits and operate at our highest and healthiest.

FRESH AIR
Breathe deeply. Fresh air is a deposit, and it conducts electricity.

WATER
Our bodies are 70 percent water, and our brains are 93 percent water. Water, particularly moving water, conducts electricity. What you drink today walks and talks tomorrow.

When we don't drink water, we get dehydration of the

brain. We call it a headache, so we take two pills with half an ounce of water. That's how backward our generation is. It's all about prescriptions, convenience, and fast food, instead of healthy, whole foods and fresh water. The point is, make deposits. Water is a deposit.

SUNSHINE

We live in this greedy era where we don't eat fruits and vegetables, we don't go in the sun, and we don't live healthy lifestyles. Instead, we go outside and put on visors, carry umbrellas, and slather on petroleum-based sunscreen that—what?—causes skin cancer.

How is it possible that we are the first generation so driven by money that we say the sun causes skin cancer? We're the first generation that has come to that conclusion. People in many cultures work their entire lives in the sun and have no cases of skin cancer.

Does the sun really cause skin cancer? Or is it a lack of fruits and vegetables in your diet? True sunscreen is called beta-carotene. You eat it. If you want sunscreen, eat a lot of fruits and vegetables. If you have fair skin and are on a healthy diet, yes, of course, use caution in the sun. Remember, moderation.

Air, water, and sunshine—these are fascinating to me. Combine the three, and you have a flower that blossoms and reaches up to the heavens. We're no different. Combine them, and nature does its miracle for us. The plant naturally synthesizes phytonutrients and phyto-chemicals in raspberries, apples, oranges, etc. Yet scientists were baffled for years because they couldn't find these nutrients in the dirt. Instead marketers told everybody that the dirt just wasn't good anymore, so we had to add some-thing to it. It's a crazy, greed-driven inferiorism.

Give a flower air, water, and sunshine and it embraces life and reaches high. We are no different.

R.W.

EXERCISE

There are a thousand ways to exercise. Walking is physi-cally good for you. It starts up the thyroid. It makes you happy. It's impossible to walk and be mad at the same time. Walking will make you feel good. We don't need more psychiatrists in this world; we need more walkers.

I love to be out and acknowledge nature. I think of a power greater than we are, and it is absolutely creative. Our job, our opportunity, and our pleasure in this life is to create. What are you creating now?

TRUST IN NATURE

I love the notion that indigenous cultures slice a carrot, and the inside looks like an eye to them. So they say carrots must be for the eye. In the same way, a walnut is an exact replica of the brain. White grapes and red grapes are good for white blood cells and red blood cells. Tomatoes and the heart are identical. Avocados, from blossom to seed, grow for forty weeks, and they are good for women. That's no coincidence. It's fascinating. Nature in its whole form is nutritionally complex so we don't have to be. That's the whole point of ForeverGreen.

RELATIONSHIPS

You can tell your victim stories and play small. You can tell how your parents, your brother, or your boss victimized you. Your boyfriend, your girlfriend, your husband, your wife. Victim, victim, victim. That's the smallest way to play life. But if you take responsibility for all your relationships, you are embracing good health. Healthy relationships are a huge part of health and well-being. Be kind. That, too, is a deposit.

PASSION

People say, "I used to dance." Why did you stop dancing? Dance, or sing, or play sports—whatever makes you happy, do it regularly. Because that is part of your health and well-being.

SPIRITUALITY

One more key, spirituality—whatever that means to you. It is something bigger than all of us, and it is the thread that runs through everything we've talked about. Spirituality makes us less carnal. It pulls us through addictions, through health, through relationships, through hard times, through life in general.

THE WORLD'S FIRST FOOD

Many of the modern world's great discoveries were made by accident. Alexander Fleming discovered penicillin when he forgot to discard some contaminated petri dishes.

When I woke up just after dawn on September 28, 1928, I certainly didn't plan to revolutionize all medicine by discovering the world's first antibiotic, or bacteria killer. But I guess that was exactly what I did.

ALEXANDER FLEMING

Wilhelm Roentgen accidentally discovered X-rays while he was conducting experiments with the radiation from cathode rays. Teflon was accidentally invented by researchers attempting to create a new refrigerant.

Tom Harper's accidental discovery of the nutritional value of marine phytoplankton may not earn him the Nobel Prize, but it is changing the world in a profound way.

Phytoplankton are microscopic free-floating ocean plants that form the base of the ocean's food chain, and there are many diverse species. Tom's discovery began in 1989, when he and his wife, Margaret, decided to buy a sea farm for shellfish on Vancouver Island in British Columbia, Canada. Tom was a fourth-generation islander, and he had seen all his life the unique opportunity afforded by the confluence of the sea with cold, clean freshwater flowing all the way from the Canadian Rockies. In the estuaries in and around the island, large shellfish grew in great abundance.

Realizing that demand for shellfish would outstrip even this abundant supply, in 1995 Tom began growing his own supply in tanks on his farm, feeding them with synthetically produced plankton, the industry standard at that time. The results were anything but spectacular. Tom's farm-grown shellfish were puny and anemic looking compared with the ones he had harvested in the wild. The answer, he theorized, was nutrition. Vancouver Island's shellfish are among the finest in the world because of an unusually abundant supply of phytoplankton in the cold waters of the Eastern Pacific Ocean, often visible from orbiting satellites. NASA scientists explain the phenomenon:

The coastal waters of the Eastern Pacific are productive because wind and ocean currents allow nutrient-rich water from deep in the ocean to rise to the surface. The cold, rising water carries phosphates and nitrates, which act as fertilizer to the phytoplankton that grow in the sunlit waters at the ocean's surface. Since phytoplankton is the base of the food chain, areas that support large phytoplankton blooms tend to have large fish populations.

Off the coast of Vancouver Island and Washington State, phytoplankton blooms tend to happen when winds blow down the coast from the north. The winds push the ocean's surface water west, out to sea. Deep water rises up to replace the wind-blown surface water, and it carries the nutrients needed to support phytoplankton blooms.

NASA EARTH OBSERVATORY
JULY 7, 2006

Tom knew that thousands of species of phytoplankton were growing in those abundant ocean waters, while the purchased supply he fed to his shellfish contained only nine species grown in synthetic seawater under synthetic sunlight. He was determined to grow and harvest wild phytoplankton in natural seawater under natural sunlight. Others before him had tried and failed to grow wild marine phytoplankton in quantities necessary to support a shellfish operation, so Tom and Margaret knew that if they succeeded, they would transform the aquaculture industry. And they were willing to risk virtually all of their assets to make it happen.

Eight years later Tom was producing more than forty metric tons of wild marine phytoplankton per day, using all of Mother Nature—natural seawater, natural sunlight, natural nutrients—for his marine phytoplankton to thrive twelve months out of the year under any weather conditions.

Another beautiful effect of Tom's operation is that marine phytoplankton consume two and a half times their weight in carbon dioxide every day and give back only oxygen. You can't get any cleaner than that. NASA tells us, in fact, that phytoplankton in the world's oceans produce as much as 90 percent of our oxygen.

It might have been possible for Tom to allow the same

phytoplankton to grow month after month in his tanks, but he knew the shellfish would perform better if the seasonal changes in the ocean were reflected in his tanks. So every month he went to sea to harvest fresh samples to serve as a starter in the tanks, and every month he returned to the sea the phytoplankton he had been growing—hundreds of times more than he had taken.

"Over time I began to see an explosion of sea life on our beach," Tom recalls. "We were putting back cleaner water than we took out, and it contained huge amounts of algae that we didn't need. There was a population explosion of clams and oysters living there, as well as California sea lions, eagles, otters, and other higher species. I began to understand the truth that marine phytoplankton forms the basis of the food chain in the ocean, and we were strengthening the entire ecosystem in our area."

Tom also experienced a similar explosion in the health of his business as he sold phytoplankton to other shellfish farmers. "The business took off in a way we never expected," he says.

As his sea farm business grew, however, Tom's own health deteriorated. Tom has diabetes, and he has experienced many of the negative impacts that go along with that disease. His family told him to slow down, as fatigue seemed to drag him down constantly. They feared he might have pneumonia. Tom finally went in for tests and learned that he had mesothelioma, a type of lung cancer related to exposure to asbestos from his many years working as a marine engineer in the shipping industry.

"They told me I had a few weeks, at most a few months, to live," Tom says, "so I started putting my affairs in order and making plans to sell the sea farm."

Tom's daughter, Tiffany Haarsma, recalls the disappointment the entire family experienced when they realized that Tom would not live to see his work come to fruition.

"At the same time," she says, "we were so proud of him because he was still out there doing what he does best, trying to improve on solutions he had found in the aquaculture industry. His inner drive is so beautiful to see—he was committed to growing and harvesting these extraordinary species of wild phytoplankton in a controlled, safe environment on land. Even when he wasn't well, he just kept going."

Tom picks up the story from there: "One day I was standing there looking into the tanks at these rich phytoplankton, and I was thinking about my health problems. I knew that medical researchers had found cures for all sorts of health problems in plants, and here I had thousands of plants that nobody has ever explored for health cures. Something inside me told me to take some phytoplankton myself. So I took a teaspoon of it and washed it down with a glass of water. The next day I did it again, and I repeated it every day. Over time I began to feel more energetic, and the pain between the pleural lining and my lungs decreased."

Tom told friends and neighbors what he had experienced, and others said they wanted to eat some of his phytoplankton. They got so excited about it, the story made the local newspaper. A ForeverGreen distributor in the area read the story and passed it along to us, thinking this might be a great product to consider distributing. I agreed, and we immediately called Tom and Tiffany, and they agreed to meet us.

FIRST IMPRESSIONS

Tiffany tells the story of our first meeting: "So many people were calling wanting to sell our product. I received a call from a leader at ForeverGreen, and I was not overly receptive to her. In fact, she called three times before I spoke with her. She said she had heard about our product from the articles, and said the president of ForeverGreen was going to be on the island. Could he meet with us?

"Well it took some convincing to allow Ron to come out. We're very protective of who we let come to the farm. But we learned enough about ForeverGreen to be comfortable with it. And with the president of the company coming, Dad and I dressed in our Sunday best.

I try to surround myself with people who at their core enjoy their job, whether it's running a doughnut shop, selling a product, or being a librarian. People who are passionate about what they do will be fantastic at it.

R.W.

"Then Ron, bless him, walks out looking like he had just walked out of a campsite. The motor home he was in had been towed, he was wearing jeans and flip-flops, and there was mustard on his shirt. Dad flashed a look at me like,

This has humbled our entire valley. Our journey is such a sacred journey—my father's in particular. So many things in his life led to this point: being born on the island, his love of the ocean, working in the marine industry all his life—all of these things led to this opportunity, even some of the bad choices he made with food and lifestyle. From a legacy standpoint, I'm really proud of my father. He's a brilliant man, my dad, and we're grateful we've been able to share marine phytoplankton through ForeverGreen because of the stand they have taken.

TIFFANY HAARSMA

'Honey, you've got to be kidding me.' Ron looked like the president of an outdoors club, not a successful company.

"Then he brought out some 24 Karat Chocolate—he knows how to reach a girl's heart—and he began to share his vision for ForeverGreen, his community stands, and his vision for wild marine phytoplankton. It was almost as though ForeverGreen had been created for us."

ALIGNING THE VISIONS

Tom and Tiffany knew they had something unique, and when I arrived, along with a couple of other ForeverGreen staff, they told me they had already met with several other companies interested in bringing marine phytoplankton to the market. Then I began to explain our vision for the future of ForeverGreen—our desire to contribute to mankind and to the earth—and in a short time our visions aligned. That was no accident.

"We wanted to make what we had found available to everyone," Tiffany says, "but we were concerned that it might attract greed rather than heart. We were looking for people with good business sense as well as heart—someone who understood how truly significant this product is.

I grew up in the Pacific Northwest and spent a lot of time on the coastline, rocks, and beaches. Being at the coast near Tom Harper's sea farm was unlike any other beach I had ever experienced. The amount of life on the beach was truly amazing. You think you're walking on rocks, but no, it's oysters and clams absolutely everywhere because of the amount of phytoplankton Tom is creating and returning to the sea. Then you go to his farm, and you experience this sense of reverence, a unique feeling knowing what Tom is creating there. It's an amazing place.

BEN ALLEN, DIRECTOR OF MARKETING

"Ron impressed us with his vision for ForeverGreen, the products they had introduced, and their stands in the community. That absolutely appealed to us."

Tom and Tiffany selected ForeverGreen to introduce marine phytoplankton to the world, and after establishing exclusivity in our industry, we then went about developing the product. A patented two-step process, relying on neither heat nor chemicals, uses pressure and benign gasses to extract the entirety of the plant—essential oils, resins, and aqueous materials—without compromising beneficial properties. This process, called aqueous molecular partitioning, makes the entire plant water-soluble and instantly bio-available. What you drink today walks and talks tomorrow. No chemicals, no emulsifiers. The body is absorbing the phytoplankton from the moment of entry into the mouth.

Then we enhanced the most efficacious material found in the marine kingdom with the highest materials from the plant kingdom: frankincense, aloe vera, rose extract, ginger, lemon, lime, blueberry, ginger, cranberry, apple, and others to create a complete food drink.

The response to our first phytoplankton product, FrequenSea, has been nothing short of amazing. What excites me most about FrequenSea is the number of people coming to ForeverGreen, because our message is to stand for one person at a time and be counted on this planet to make a difference. If you make a difference today, you change the world. But it's hard to be counted when you're sick. You cannot create and sustain your dreams in life if you're stepping over your health and are sick.

The body is a self-healing mechanism. It will perform miracles by the minute when we learn to honor and edify its intelligence. And based on the results, nothing honors and edifies the body like FrequenSea with marine phytoplankton.

———————————————

Belief creates activity.

Activity creates volume.

Volume creates bigger checks.

Bigger checks substantiate more belief.

It's as simple as that. That is the magic equation
of network marketing.

RICK REDFORD, VICE PRESIDENT OF GLOBAL SALES

———————————————

I had been working for another major company in the industry for thirteen years when I
heard about ForeverGreen. I had known Ron
Williams many years earlier, and when I heard
about his philosophy for ForeverGreen and
what its products are all about, I knew I had to
join them. In 2007 I left behind thirteen years
with another company to take the next step for
myself. It's the best decision I ever made.

JORGE E. ALVARADO
VICE PRESIDENT OF LATIN AMERICAN BUSINESS DEVELOPMENT

OPPORTUNITY

When everyone does a little, we all win big.

—

R.W.

ANCHOR AN opportunity with a larger cause and purpose, and all of the sudden you find reasons to succeed that are greater than just paying bills. Good action in the community actually feeds your bottom line. So when we say we're staking flags in the ground with timeless principles of health and community, then ForeverGreen truly is a way of being—one person at a time.

The cause and purpose anchoring those opportunities makes ForeverGreen different. If an opportunity becomes hollow, you're reduced to asking, "What's the product?" and "What's the compensation plan?" After a while that mind-set brings out the lowest form of behavior, because you convince yourself that your product stinks and you stink. People who hype hollow opportunities with bright colors, pyrotechnics, and balloons never have an anchor. They come and they go, drifting with the flow of whatever is going on around them. If it's only flash and cash, it doesn't fit in here. We're not much into the hype that goes along with that. We try not to get overly jazzed. Keeping it real and waiting for the long-term truth to emerge is more important to us. So is maintaining relationships. I've worked for several companies, and I've kept friendly relationships with all of them. I haven't made as much money as others in this industry who took shorter roads, but I believe when you sell your soul up front, there is always a price to pay.

Creating and fulfilling opportunity is about your hands, your heart, and your mind—never forgetting the tremendous financial opportunity. We remain keen to business and the fundamentals of execution; otherwise the

A lot of industries are struggling through economic turmoil. Network marketing is one of the places where the more unstable the economy is, the more opportunity there is for building the business. The more people are looking for additional income, the more opportunity you have to recruit people to hear the message.

TIM SIMPSON, CHIEF INFORMATION OFFICER

Learning

Determined

Successful

Part-Time

Full-Time

Free

Rainmaker

Ron and I started meeting and creating plans for getting ForeverGreen underway. We were talking products and philosophy; then he explained compensation plan rankings.

At that moment, when he put those titles on that white board, I knew I wanted to be involved in ForeverGreen. He was approaching titles from a substantive principle-based behavior communication place—not medals or gemstones. What does a medal mean? The Olympics value gold and silver. But Ron is focused on behavior and helping people achieve their dreams and desires—teaching them how to get there through the smallest details. He's so thorough and layered in his thinking, and that leads us all to be part of a team, to take vision and make it tangible.

CRAIG SMITH, DIRECTOR OF COMMUNITY STANDS

---

vision becomes fraud. If we're going to work hard, then let's get paid for it. The ForeverGreen philosophy is about sustaining good health and financial independence, and promoting kindness along the way. There is no reason we can't promote social well-being in our professional lives and earn residual income doing it.

As I write this book, the United States and the world are experiencing the greatest economic scare since the Great Depression. Millions of people are using fear as an excuse to fail. They're even allowing their children to suffer.

At the same time, nearly fifty thousand people a day join our industry, building home-based businesses and stepping through their fear to build our own economy. They're learning that the multilevel marketing industry is recession-proof, and that we can either refuse to give our power to the "bad economy" or use the economy as an excuse to fail. We in this industry choose to create our own economy. When everyone does a little, we create big results.

These are the people who have made ForeverGreen the success it is and made direct sales the most intelligent form of income generation. They have created and fulfilled their dreams by becoming the authors of their own lives and by living a life of design rather than default. When you embrace all that ForeverGreen can be, it becomes a place where you want to live, not just pop in and out of.

BREAKING THE MOLD

To put into perspective the opportunity offered by our industry, and especially ForeverGreen, I have to go back to that little apartment where I grew up with my brothers and sister. In fact, to create a video for ForeverGreen, we took a camera there, and it was like a magnet. One minute a kid was looking through a wrought-iron gate at us, and in the blink of an eye, a dozen more appeared. It was like going to another country, where I was the foreigner and the curious children wanted to know more. And yet, this was the place where I had grown up. Not so long ago I was one of those kids playing under these same trees—a place where our "mall" was the sound of the ice cream man. That was our shopping experience. I think my mother purposely didn't take us shopping because we might lose sleep over the things we saw but could not have.

I looked at the layers of apartments and saw how we'd been packed in there, and I was humbled. At the same time, I was filled with gratitude for all I had—the learnings, failures, and successes. And I was reminded once again that life is a process, and we live it in different phases. That is what ForeverGreen is about. This is where my season began, and I am grateful.

The contrast reminded me that network marketing is the greatest form of free enterprise on earth, giving each of us—even a kid like me—the opportunity to control our destiny and to break the mold.

At a certain point as a teenager I consciously broke the mold. I remember thinking, *I've got to do something different from the generations around me.* When you're living paycheck-to-paycheck, when it's so hard to make the rent, when you never have the privilege of seeing your mother and father interact and you can't see what marriage looks like, well, you can imagine what the expectations were for us as kids. In fact, I don't think we even had any expectations.

I decided that whatever I was going to be, I was going to throw myself into it completely, if only for the sake of creating a higher standard in the next generation. I always had big visions, even in my childhood. I was not consciously aware then that I had big visions, but looking back I can't remember small visions. When we have big visions,

—————————————

I love this industry. It is way of life for many millions of people. I believe ForeverGreen has a mission to transform the industry in such a way that every person who gets into such a novel business as this is also taking a stand for the community. That's something Ron has always done. I believe it will be even more beautiful as we are perceived as a community of givers—giving of ourselves to the community to make a difference, one person at a time. I believe ForeverGreen dignifies the industry.

JORGE E. ALVARADO
VICE PRESIDENT OF LATIN AMERICAN BUSINESS DEVELOPMENT

—————————————

our circumstances don't matter. We can discover a way to manifest the visions in our lives.

My mom tells the story of a promise I made to her when I was nine years old and I got my first guitar. "Mom," she remembers me saying, "when I get big I'm going to be a millionaire. I'm gonna make money, buy you a house, get you a maid, and give you $5,000 a month to spend. I mean it, Mom."

At nine years old I had been given a purpose that would be the anchor for everything I do—the love my mother had poured out on me and had taught me to share. I was already committed.

Some people think commitment is an emotion. It is not. Either you are committed or you are not. You cannot be more or less committed. Commitment is holding true to the decisions you have made, even the emotional decisions, after the emotion is gone. The idea of being committed and keeping your word is everything. It's the foundation to anyone's longevity in business, family, friendships, and relationships. I love the story of Hernando Cortez, who landed near the site of Veracruz, Mexico, in 1519 and immediately had his ships burned so there would be no thought of retreat. That's commitment!

The easiest thing to do in network marketing is quit. You're out there on an island in some small city, and one day it's not working for you so, *boom*, you're done. You're going to quit. If you have a rough day, and your emphasis is this product or this dollar, that's when you're likely to bounce around in this industry. That's when you say, "The company let me down. The company hurt me. The company preached an idea that was too good to be true."

To succeed you have to break that mold and set a standard and embrace a vision and a purpose that's bigger than all of us. Then, when that logistical challenge arises, you don't have a hollow commitment that might allow you to quit.

ForeverGreen has mastered creating a vision, a mission, and a purpose bigger than all of us, so that during a rough day, you know you're going to be okay, because there's something bigger that we're engaged in.

REALITY AND HOPE

You may have read the previous section and thought, *That's easy for Ron to say. Look at how successful ForeverGreen is.* It hasn't always been so. Our commitment has been thoroughly tested.

————————————————

When we evaluate a new product we always keep several things in mind: Is it healthy? Is it the highest quality we can find? Is it unique? Can we take it to the marketplace effectively? Does it align with our vision to enhance the lives of others?

BRENDA HUANG, CHIEF MARKETING OFFICER

————————————————

The summer before we launched FrequenSea, a ForeverGreen distributor called our office to sign up someone. A week later she called to sign someone else up, and then told Robert Reitz, our senior vice president of business analysis, "This number is only ten higher than last week. Did you only sign up ten people in a week?"

Robert couldn't deny it. We had some slow summer weeks in those days, and yes, we had only signed up ten distributors since her previous call.

We were selling chocolate and hormone cream and were intentionally adding products a few at a time. Over the first couple of years, sales had grown slowly every month, and an investor we were relying on to help fund the company was concerned that sales were not growing fast enough. He became reluctant to continue the funding.

"I've invested a lot in the company already," he said, "and I don't see a return coming."

We were at a critical point where we needed additional money to launch a new product, and he said no. Period.

What followed was an intense negotiation between the investor and me. I explained how the additional investment would be the last one ForeverGreen would need, and without it we would miss out on an important opportunity. He stood firm.

Those were difficult days for the staff because we knew ForeverGreen was on the verge of becoming phenomenally successful; we just hadn't gotten there. The company was growing well but not funding itself. So the staff came to me and offered to take a pay cut if that would free up the money to launch the new product. It was a huge commitment on their part, and an amazing statement of confidence in our products and our purpose.

We all knew that wouldn't be enough, but when I told our investor that the employees were ready to sacrifice for the company, he generously agreed to invest more.

So in the summer of 2005, Brenda Huang, Ben Allen, and I went on a tour to introduce the product, a chocolate weight-loss drink. Midway through the tour, sales were going well, though not great.

Robert recalls how difficult those days were back at headquarters: "In the middle of the trip, Ron and I were talking on the phone, and I was wondering if we're going to have to start laying off employees, or even shut down the company. They were the darkest days of my life. I was showing up to work, and it was hard to walk through the door. I knew there was a future for us, but it was getting

People at ForeverGreen see in me my true potential, and I am able to do the same for others—
hold them up to their best selves. We've created
a space within ForeverGreen where we're able
to create the best potential. Doing that has
allowed me to become a better husband, better
father, better son, better brother, better coworker.

CHRIS PATTERSON
CHIEF OPERATING OFFICER AND GENERAL COUNSEL

hard to see—like I was sitting in a black liquid. Everything around felt like it was closing in."

Brenda, Ben, and I were heading out toward western Canada for a meeting that Marilyn Stewart, one of our first distributors, was putting together, when she called to tell me about "this incredible, possibly self-sustaining, food that is getting out to people on Vancouver Island." She was talking about marine phytoplankton, and she arranged for us to meet with Tom Harper and Tiffany Haarsma at Tom's farm. After the meeting I immediately called Robert and told him we had just met an amazing person with an amazing story and an amazing product that would take ForeverGreen to the next level. Robert tried not to be openly skeptical.

"I've learned that you have to listen to Ron," he says today. "He has a mind that is much more wide open than most of us. He sees huge pictures and amazing ideas. Still, it sometimes takes him a little while to bring you into the *why* of his amazing ideas. So he's telling me on the phone from Canada about marine phytoplankton, and I'm saying, 'Great, Ron. Sounds like you're excited, and I'm sure I'll be excited.' But I'm not getting excited over the phone."

We were two weeks away from a conference with our top leaders, and I knew we had to launch this new product

With Ron, it's not about management style but about leadership. He cares about all of us sincerely. People feel that and want to do something for him. We never operate out of fear but out of abundant loving. Ron says, "Let's do this together," and when we get on the same page to do it, the sky's the limit.

DAYLEN BUSHMAN
VICE PRESIDENT OF MANUFACTURING AND FULFILLMENT

at that time. Not only that, but we were going to create the new brand, make a movie, have boxes designed and printed. Robert was wondering how in the world we were going to pull that off. "Ron," he said, "there's only thirteen of us on staff. It's not going to happen."

"We can do this," I said. "We will do this. It's going to be amazing!"

We returned to Utah and started putting together the launch of FrequenSea. I started calling our distributors and enrolling them with this idea of a great new product without telling them anything about it. I knew, though, that this product would take ForeverGreen to a new level.

In the meantime, the staff was pulling all the pieces together to create the product, the packaging, the movie, and the meeting. Before that year our annual convention had been twenty or thirty people. We didn't even book a room; we just met at the ForeverGreen headquarters.

As we raced to pull everything together, we had a hundred distributors show up. Every chair in the room was taken, and people were standing all around the sides and out in the hallway. I walked in with the catalog that has all of our product lines, and everyone was cheering. They love our products. Then I held it up and dropped it on the floor.

ForeverGreen is about bringing out of us what we are inside, going about every moment making a difference in our lives, taking responsibility for our actions. It's a way of being—as simple as that.

PAUL FRAMPTON, CHIEF FINANCIAL OFFICER

"That's your safety net," I said. "You'll always have those products you love. But what you're about to see will create a rocket for ForeverGreen."

Then we wheeled in a pyramid stack of FrequenSea, and I told the amazing story of Tom Harper, the sea farm, and phytoplankton. We showed the video, and the room was absolutely silent. They were awestruck at the possibilities of telling this story to the world.

We're creating tools for distributors to build relationships and build their business.

BEN ALLEN, DIRECTOR OF MARKETING

In two weeks we had pulled it off, and distributors had this amazing movie they could mail or put on a Web site.

Just like that we went from the dark days of our investor not wanting to put more money into ForeverGreen to our first three days of FrequenSea sales, which almost doubled the previous three months' sales combined. Sales continued to grow 10 percent a month,

———————————

Network marketing is relationship marketing. It's about people, not stuff. Marketing never comes first. Relationships come first. Marketing simply allows distributors to have the tools they need to go out and work.

RICK REDFORD, VICE PRESIDENT OF GLOBAL SALES

———————————

then 10 percent more, then 30 percent more, and on and on until our sales grew ten times in ten months.

SHARED OPPORTUNITIES, SHARED RESPONSIBILITIES

Every network marketing company relies completely on its distributors. That's why the word *network* comes first in our industry. At our headquarters we continue to build an organization designed to meet the distributors' needs and ensure their success.

Some people do business with a poker face—they get the quick hit, get out, and don't care who gets hurt along the way. Those people are just poisoning humanity and taking away from the belief system in mankind. Anybody can go into a room and light it up and then leave. My attempt in front of the room is to get the facts straight and be authentically felt. I don't want a lot of bright balloons and pyrotechnics. Just get the facts right and be felt—with passion and enthusiasm. Enthusiasm is great as long as it's authentic, but the measure of success—the measure of character—is whether you can help someone find happiness over time. To do that you have to come down from the skybox onto the field where you can play the game alongside the team—where you can sweat, bleed, and lose sleep with them while you build your shared success.

We believe that if you can enhance the belief system of humankind by creating an experience for your customers, distributors, and employees, that is above and beyond fundamental business, that's what it's all about.

That's why the blueprint for our business model is a high standard of consciousness in the company and the expectation of a high level of corporate responsibility. We are very much about humanity and coexisting in spite of our differences. We are not a company of dictators but of responsible people who are equal, just with different responsibilities. No job is bigger or smaller than any other. They are all equally important, from the receptionist to the president. We set up platforms for people to be heard so they don't have to whisper in a corner of the hall or the bathroom or the break room. If we have a problem, we throw it out on the table. Nobody says, "That's not my problem," or "That's not my department." We deal with it, clean it up, get back into alignment, and all go home happy. Anyone at any time has a vote or can stand up and make a point. We all have a voice and we make decisions together. When we all align on idea, concept, or purpose, that is our trade secret. That is our power. Alignment supersedes mechanism. We believe this is the new model for a successful business—acknowledging the realness of humanity yet also the clear and concise fundamentals of executing a business.

How much of ForeverGreen is about a guy like me who has a vision and takes a stand, and how much of it is about empowerment? That's always the biggest challenge for me: how much do I put into it and how much do I pull back and empower others? Obviously my answer is, "I'll know when that time is, when people are taking it on themselves."

It's fun to sit in my chair and see how many people come in and make it happen versus the people who come in and complain. You can see a correlation between their language, their worldviews, their actions, and their results. It's a great lesson to see how many people make it work. Most of the time it's no accident that people show up at certain times. The message you're putting out in the world will attract people who find that message interesting, and repel the ones who do not. Then your people become your best recruiters. If you have good

Ninety percent of the time Ron is driven, sharp, articulating what he wants. When he's running the business, he's focused. His humor is the sprinkle on top. Some employees are very serious, and they may be having a very difficult time, and Ron will come cruising through the office wearing a tribal outfit. That's his way of telling you to take a break. Take a breather, and don't get another headache. He's not ignoring your stress; he's acknowledging it and showing his love. If you could choose between a serious boss and a crazy boss, most people would choose a crazy boss.

BRENDA HUANG, CHIEF MARKETING OFFICER

employees, hire their friends. If you're a good place to work, they'll do the recruiting. If your employees are not telling their friends they ought to be working with you, maybe something's wrong.

If you're looking for something real, something true, get up off the couch and join arms with an indiscriminate global community who wants to be counted one person at a time. Your hands and mine. I invite you to take a stand with us, and let's get on with it.

A WORLD OF OPPORTUNITY

In our commitment to remain in stage one of the corporate lifecycle, we introduced a new family of weight-management products, O3World. These appetite-control products are different from anything we have offered at ForeverGreen, and they provide an introduction to everything we offer.

If whole foods were the only the solution for weight loss, we'd have a line outside our manufacturing facility every day. But for most overweight people—and that is two-thirds of Americans, or 200 million people—the problem is willpower. O3World products put people in

Typical Corporate Lifecycle

Stage one: This is the creative stage where we lose sleep because we are so filled with passion for what we are doing. We go to bed with a smile and wake up with happy feet.

Stage two: Then the company moves into maintenance mode, where it tries to hold onto the wealth it has created.

Stage three: That lends self to heavy-handed policies and procedures—lists of all the things we can't do. When what we resist persists, we end up in . . .

Stage four: Litigation and heartbreak. Our commitment at ForeverGreen is to stay in the creative mode, stage one, always developing and introducing new concepts and new ways to show them to the world—always prepared for growth.

control of their portions, helping them make decisive, not compulsive, eating habits. That's a big deal today. And when the compulsion to eat is replaced by a decision, people make healthier choices. ForeverGreen is there with our lineup of healthy whole foods.

When we launched O3World, we started signing up hundreds of people a day, thousands in the first month. People joined and generated more sales and more people selling, and it continues to build on itself.

With the explosion in sales we are experiencing, we are in touch with more people and branching out to more countries. We've grown at a pace that allows us to go into and support new markets the way they need to be supported. The timing couldn't be better.

The other great thing about the timing is that we have the experience and organization as a company to support the exciting growth. I've been involved in and seen other companies that went straight up, and a good portion of those sales fell straight down because the companies hadn't built a solid foundation. We've created sustainable growth, even at this accelerated pace, because we have the right people and systems in place.

With ForeverGreen, and especially with the O3World product line, we are seeing people from all walks of life and all social spectrums coming to this opportunity because they need the health benefits of managing their weight without spending twenty hours a week in the gym, as well as financial opportunities to make their life better. A number of distributors, after years of comfort with their residual income, are engaged again because of the introduction of O3World. While they may not have issues with weight management, they know enough people who do, and they're picking up O3 and running with it.

TIM SIMPSON, CHIEF INFORMATION OFFICER

HAPPY CHILDREN

My story began with my daughter; now let me end it with all of the sons and daughters and the opportunity we have to make a difference in their lives. Every three seconds, somewhere around the world, a child dies from starvation or dehydration. Yet, the money we spend annually in America on weight loss alone is twice the amount of money needed to feed the world's hungry each year. At ForeverGreen we created the Happy Children Foundation, a nonprofit organization reaching out to children worldwide. Whether it is feeding, clothing, educating, or medically treating children, the Happy Children Foundation is there. We provide real, simple meals, with twenty-six whole-food ingredients. Just add water and you have calories and nutrition.

At the other end of the spectrum, we are committed to the overall general health of kids, teens, and young adults. This includes education, prevention, and solutions to addictions of all kinds, childhood obesity, and malnutrition.

We worked with schools to create the Power Lunch program, and I got to go into schools with good whole foods—fresh fruits and vegetables—and the kids loved it.

They lined up for apples, bananas, and grapes. They love fresh food and they know instinctively that it's better for them. Ben Allen designed posters and had hundreds of them printed to put in school lunchrooms as part of our campaign to educate kids on the value of good foods. School leaders were excited to see that if they provide healthy food, kids will eat it.

So many opportunities to experience and share health, kindness, and opportunity . . . and with a network of people around me to make the most of each of them, we are all embracing every second of every season of our lives. Welcome home.

ome a "Big Brother" for a young person... Jason K., San Diego
ska Connect schools with the Power Lunch program... Misty V.
nnesota Teach children financial literacy... Jim & Audrey S
nielle B., Lovell, Wyoming Clean up the schoolyard... Kenne
Bountiful, Utah Shovel more than my walk when it snows...
.. Ronsi S., Westcliffe, Colorado Work with recovering alcoh
Girls Club"... Linda B., Greeley, Colorado Be a mentor for "h
he homeless each month... Nadene V., Las Vegas, Nevada
sconsin Teach exercise at senior centers... Russel M., Salt Lake
e school and health supplies to Mexico... Cara-Leigh M., Calg
draising for musical instruments... Amelia G., Vancouver, I
rie, Wisconsin Build an international tennis academy... Tho
drea S., Lethbridge, Alberta Visit prison inmates... Anthony A

WHAT'S YO

lins, Colorado Play with animals at the shelter... Andrea M
hbridge, Alberta Reach out to drug addicts... Bill S., Glenda
e blood every month... Michael L., Scottsdale, Arizona Help
.. Tadayoshi K., Tokyo, Japan Send a bouquet of flowers to so
homes... Dorothy G., Albany, New York Volunteer at an orph
Fairfield, Iowa Teach a parenting skills class... Janelle L., Prov
rth Carolina Become trained in emergency and disaster resp
hmond, Wisconsin Volunteer to hold pre-mature babies... Jo
ewood, Ohio Educate low-income people on growing garden
ghbors... Janeen R., Monroe, Utah Create a dance program for
lters... Karen L., Coaldale, Colorado Smile at everyone I me
t mothers... Julie B., Minneapolis, Minnesota "Adopt" a senio
m... Barabara A., Wyomissing, Pennsylvania Read to children